TRINITY GUILDHALL

D1439346

Drum Kit 4

WITHDRAWN

Pieces & Studies
for Trinity Guildhall examinations
2011–2013

Grades 7 & 8

ABERDEEN COLLEGE
GALLOWGATE LIBRARY
01224 612138

Published by
Trinity College London
89 Albert Embankment
London SE1 7TP UK

T +44 (0)20 7820 6100
F +44 (0)20 7820 6161
E music@trinityguildhall.co.uk
www.trinityguildhall.co.uk

Copyright © 2010 Trinity College London
First impression, June 2010

Unauthorised photocopying is illegal.

No part of this publication may be copied or reproduced in any
form or by any means without the prior permission of the publisher.

Printed in England by Halstan & Co. Ltd, Amersham, Bucks.

114324
Aberdeen College Library

Trinity Guildhall graded drum kit examinations

Introduction

The role of the drum kit player is a multifaceted one; drummers are required to play a multitude of styles (and often instruments) with conviction, flair and musical confidence. In show and cabaret playing, drummers are also required to have the ability to read and improvise. Stylistic versatility is essential to a drum kit player: the Latin American and African rhythms that are becoming increasingly influential and popular in contemporary music, strict tempo ballroom styles, contemporary pop and rock, not to mention jazz and funk, all need to be assessed. The strength of the Trinity Guildhall drum kit syllabus lies in not only challenging candidates, but in developing them towards becoming accomplished musicians.

In today's performing arena, drum kit playing is 90% accompaniment and 10% solo. It is therefore the aim of the Trinity Guildhall examination system to reflect this and to cover as broad a style base as possible over the eight grades.

Rudiment playing is assessed in a stylistic way, with candidates performing rudimental studies pertinent to the instrument. Rudiments are presented progressively for each grade and stylistic studies are performed as separate musical entities alongside the pieces.

Drum kit examinations

Candidates are required to perform:

- a rudimental study (or studies)
- one piece from Group A (played with a backing track)
- one piece from Group B (unaccompanied)
- two supporting tests

Please refer to the current syllabus for details of supporting tests.

Rudimental studies are specially written pieces that involve all the rudiments set for a particular grade (see cumulative rudiments grid). These rudiments are set out at the beginning of each grade section. Candidates will be required to learn these in order to be able to play the study (or studies).

Group A pieces have full backing accompaniment on CD with click track where appropriate, but no drums. Candidates will be marked on their ability to interpret a typical drum chart and interact with the backing in terms of time-keeping, phrasing, soloing etc.

Group B pieces are unaccompanied.

Venue equipment

At Public Centres where percussion examinations are accepted, Trinity Guildhall will normally supply a good quality five-piece drum kit that comprises:

- snare drum with adjustable drum kit (not orchestral) stand
- bass drum (18-22")
- ride cymbal (18-22")
- splash for Grades 5-8
- 3 toms (minimum) high/medium/low
- hi hat (12-14")
- crash cymbal (14-18")
- adjustable drum stool

In the case of an Examiner Visit, the visit organiser is responsible for providing the drum kit.

Drum heads should be in good condition and tuned correctly, and all stands and pedals should be in good mechanical order. Larger kits may be used, as may flat drum kits, but electric drum kits may not. Double bass drum pedals may be used in solos and fills if desired. Candidates wishing to use their own kits may only do so at the discretion of the Centre Representative, and the setting up of the kit must not be allowed to interfere with the timing of the session.

In all cases candidates must provide their own sticks, which must be in good condition and suitable for the repertoire being performed. When the examination entry is made, it should be clearly indicated on the entry form if a drum kit candidate is left handed.

For all drum kit grades it is the responsibility of the person signing the entry form to ensure that suitable playback equipment for CDs is provided. Some centres may provide this equipment and the applicant should contact the centre well in advance to confirm the arrangements. In all cases, arrangements (about power supply, equipment insurance etc.) must be agreed with the Centre Representative.

The equipment must be of good quality, comprising CD player with track search facility and good quality loudspeakers that are capable of reproducing the volume required for comfortable playalong (c. 20W). 'Ghetto blasters' are to be discouraged unless they have sufficient power to enable comfortable monitoring of CD for playalong or are connected to an external amplifier. Headphones may be worn by the candidate as long as there is a separate amplification route that enables the examiner to hear both drum kit and backing adequately.

Please note that a percussion-equipped warm-up room is not supplied for percussion examinations.

Trinity Guildhall recommends the use of ear defenders by candidates and examiners for the performance of drum kit repertoire for health and safety reasons. These should be used for all pieces and studies.

Drum kit rudiments

Rudiment / Grade	Grade 1	Grade 2	Grade 3	Grade 4	Grade 5	Grade 6	Grade 7	Grade 8
Single strokes	✓	✓	✓	✓	✓	✓	✓	✓
Double strokes	✓	✓	✓	✓	✓	✓	✓	✓
Single paradiddle	✓	✓	✓	✓	✓	✓	✓	✓
Flam		✓	✓	✓	✓	✓	✓	✓
Drag		✓	✓	✓	✓	✓	✓	✓
Four stroke ruff		✓	✓	✓	✓	✓	✓	✓
Five stroke roll			✓	✓	✓	✓	✓	✓
Seven stroke roll			✓	✓	✓	✓	✓	✓
Nine stroke roll			✓	✓	✓	✓	✓	✓
Flam tap				✓	✓	✓	✓	✓
Flam accent				✓	✓	✓	✓	✓
Flamacue				✓	✓	✓	✓	✓
Flam paradiddle				✓	✓	✓	✓	✓
Double paradiddle				✓	✓	✓	✓	✓
Paradiddle-diddle				✓	✓	✓	✓	✓
Drag and stroke					✓	✓	✓	✓
Double drag and stroke					✓	✓	✓	✓
Drag paradiddle					✓	✓	✓	✓
Single ratamacue					✓	✓	✓	✓
Double ratamacue					✓	✓	✓	✓
Triple ratamacue					✓	✓	✓	✓
Triple paradiddle						✓	✓	✓
Reverse paradiddle						✓	✓	✓
Pata fla fla							✓	✓
Swiss army triplet							✓	✓
Inward paradiddle							✓	✓

WITHDRAWN

Drum kit notation key

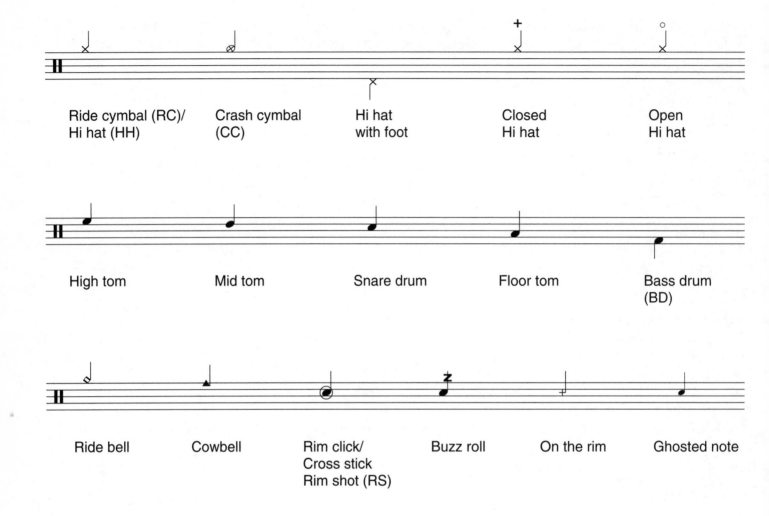

Ride cymbal (RC)/ Hi hat (HH)   Crash cymbal (CC)   Hi hat with foot   Closed Hi hat   Open Hi hat

High tom   Mid tom   Snare drum   Floor tom   Bass drum (BD)

Ride bell   Cowbell   Rim click/ Cross stick Rim shot (RS)   Buzz roll   On the rim   Ghosted note

Performance notes

General note for both grades

Where a crash cymbal appears at the start of a bar and is followed by one-bar repeat signs ([repeat sign]), the crash cymbal should **not** be played in the repeat bars. This is universally accepted as standard drum kit notation and it is the aim of the Trinity Guildhall syllabus to encourage students to become familiar with what they will be confronted with in the real world of drum kit performance.

All repeats, including those within *da capo* and *dal segno* sections, should be observed in drum kit examinations.

Grade 7

Paul Francis $\frac{3}{4}$ Workout no. 1 & no. 2 (Rudimental Studies)

Before attempting to play the whole of each piece, spend some time just playing the first two bars of time to create the right feel. Then work on one rudiment at a time before finally playing right through.

Troy Miller   Traveller

Try to catch the subtleties in this piece and make the ghost notes really quiet. The improvised solo section can be as free as you like as long as the focus is the piano. You can feel this piece as a triplet $\frac{4}{4}$.

Recommended listening: Elvin Jones on *A Love Supreme* by John Coltrane.

George Double   Lazybones

This, as the title suggests is a lazy, half-swung groove. Let the patterns breathe whilst keeping the crotchet/quarter note absolute to give the time an adequate sense of intent. Work hard to project with both feet during the ensemble section.

Rick Hudson/
Alan Barnes   Blakesley Avenue

This piece is based on a typical jazz standard format, with an additional tag at the end. The instrumental solo section has a swing feel throughout, except for the tag which returns to the original Latin groove. The Latin groove used from bar 9 is a rhythm that Art Blakey featured on many of his recordings.

Andrew Tween   Present and Correct

The underlying concept of this piece comes from Steve Gadd's drums solo piece *Crazy Army*. With this in mind, *Present and Correct* tries to use compositional ideas and playing styles from Steve Gadd's overall drumming style.

Bar 34 is an example of an inward paradiddle between the snare and cowbell.
Bar 39 is a six stroke-roll idea split between the snare, high tom, floor tom and bass drum.
Bar 49 is like a Swiss Triplet but without the flam.
Drags, five stroke and seven stroke rolls appear in the section up to bar 25.

The space between the notes is as important as the notes themselves. Give attention to the pulse so the phrases sit well without rushing the tempo.

Rolls should be clean, using open double strokes. Look to control any flamming between the bass drum and snare. Left-handed kit players can reverse the sticking where appropriate.

Neil Robinson   Off Limits

A syncopated funk solo evoking the Boogaloo and Deep Funk style from the late 1960s and early 1970s.

There should be clear distinction between the ghosted notes and accented notes on the snare. Use the left hand for the open hi hats in the closing section (bars 28-30) so the ride and open hi hat are played together.

It is really important to try and achieve a solid funky feel for this piece as well as the technical side.

Stevie Smith   For Art's Sake

This piece has a strong funk influence throughout and uses many idiomatic quotes and references. Ghost note dynamics are essential to generate the correct feel. A strong dance groove that swings is required at letter D. Letter E offers the opportunity to solo around the rhythmic figures. The 'hits' can be orchestrated any way that you like. The cascara pattern in bar 72 is to be played by clicking the sticks together above the snare drum.

Grade 8

Andrew Tween   Bo Diddley (Rudimental Study)

Bo Diddley takes a journey into the 26 rudimental requirements for Grade 8, applying them to the discipline of the drum kit. Using the framework of a 3:2 son clave or 'Bo Diddley' rhythm, this piece pushes the boundaries of coordination using polyrhythms (one time against another) and rudiments between the hands and feet. The piece is highly technical, requiring good skills of stick control and timing.

Ralph Salmins   Overture

This is a typical overture from a variety show. Keep everything bright, very energetic, and try to exaggerate all accents to make the performance as punchy as possible. The 'show 2' feel is crisp and tight and the mambo is a two-feel-showbiz style. Keep the $\frac{12}{8}$ as in the groove as possible and make the swing finisher really count with a razzy end fill.

Paul Clarvis   Lindsay's Umbrella Dance

Think of the bars of 7 as groups of two 2s and a 3, rather than a string of even semiquavers/sixteenth notes. Memorise the tune, this will help to give your playing buoyancy and musical relevance. Try to give a feeling of space in the music. It should sound energetic, but not frantic.

Recommended listening: Ivo Papasov and Orquestra Mahatma.

Luke Wastell   Purple Pumpkin

Bars 9-16: The three stroke buzz roll should be played with the left hand, with the snare drum on beat 4 played with the right hand.

Bars 17-36: The tambourine should be played with the right hand whilst the left hand carries on the drum kit pattern.

Bar 36, beats 3 & 4: Player should replace tambourine with stick.

Bars 37-end: All tom hits on the fourth semiquaver/sixteenth note of beat 3 should be played with the left hand with beat 4 (snare) played with the right hand.

Bars 53–56: The solo should be in keeping with the style of the piece.

Recommended listening: Calvin Harris, Eric Prydz and David Guetta.

Pete Riley   7evens

This piece begins with a $\frac{4}{4}$ feel that implies $\frac{7}{8}$, before eventually morphing into $\frac{7}{8}$. Throughout the piece, over the barline phrasing ideas are used, starting with emphasising crotchets/quarter notes on the bell to create a two-bar pattern and moving onto three-note groupings, played as a shuffle rhythm through the semiquavers/sixteenth notes, to create a three-bar pattern.

The ideas presented can be heard in the vocabulary of drummers such as Vinnie Colaiuta, Danny Carey and Gavin Harrison, and whilst proving challenging should also offer some interesting ways of approaching odd time signatures.

Troy Miller   Swiss Swagger

This piece is a triplet-based exercise which will help develop your left hand. It also makes use of the Swiss army triplet. Consolidating the sticking will help a great deal with the fluidity of the performance. Try and make your feet the focus when playing.

Recommended listening: Weather Report and The Meters.

Mark Schulman   Super High Five

In 2001, I received a piece of music called $\frac{5}{4}$ *Eddie* written by a brilliant bass player friend of mine, J K Kleutgens. This song in $\frac{5}{4}$ inspired an entire fusion band to form called Fusion Folk. We played some gigs around the Los Angeles area at places like the Baked Potato. This song has always been special to me and has been a favourite performance piece of mine at my drum seminars for the last few years. *Super High Five* is inspired by that piece and my love for fusion.

Grades 7 and 8 Rudiments

You will need to learn the rudiments up to Grade 6 and the following to be able to play the Rudimental Studies for Grades 7 and 8.

Pata fla fla

Swiss army triplet

Inward paradiddle

If you are left handed you may reverse the sticking.

$\frac{3}{4}$ Workout no. 1
(Grade 7 Rudimental Study no. 1)

Paul Francis

* Optional splash and closed hi hat.

Remember to look at the Performance Notes on pages 5-6

Track 2

¾ Workout no. 2
(Grade 7 Rudimental Study no. 2)

Paul Francis

Remember to look at the Performance Notes on pages 5-6

Traveller

Troy Miller

Remember to look at the Performance Notes on pages 5-6

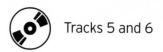

Lazybones

George Double

* HH splash with foot.

Play with dynamics appropriate to the music.

Remember to look at the Performance Notes on pages 5-6

Blakesley Avenue

Rick Hudson/Alan Barnes

Remember to look at the Performance Notes on pages 5-6

Present and Correct

Andrew Tween

The slash through the note stem indicates double strokes.

Remember to look at the Performance Notes on pages 5-6

You may photocopy this page to avoid a page turn.

This page has been left blank to facilitate page turns.

Track 10

Off Limits

♩ = 104

Neil Robinson

Remember to look at the Performance Notes on pages 5-6

* = play RC and HH together.

For Art's Sake

Stevie Smith

Remember to look at the Performance Notes on pages 5-6

ABERDEEN COLLEGE
GALLOWGATE LIBRARY

You may photocopy this page to avoid a page turn.

You may photocopy this page to avoid a page turn.

Bo Diddley
(Grade 8 Rudimental Study)

Andrew Tween

Remember to look at the Performance Notes on pages 5-6

You may photocopy this page to avoid a page turn.

Overture

Ralph Salmins

= performer's choice of drum(s) to be played using rhythm shown.

Remember to look at the Performance Notes on pages 5-6

You may photocopy this page to avoid a page turn.

Lindsay's Umbrella Dance

Paul Clarvis

* The drum sounds chosen should be appropriate to the style of the music.

You may photocopy this page to avoid a page turn.

* The **Fine** is at the end of the third semiquaver of bar 53. The notes in brackets are not played on the D.S.

Remember to look at the Performance Notes on pages 5-6

Purple Pumpkin

Luke Wastell

can be played on crash or splash cymbal at player's discretion.

The Cowbell should be mounted/attached to the kit in a place convenient to the player.

Remember to look at the Performance Notes on pages 5-6

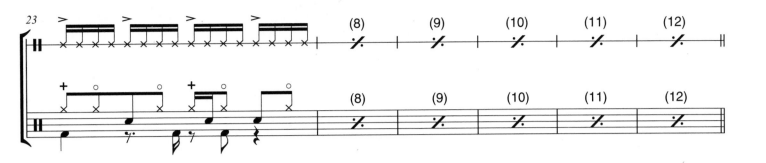

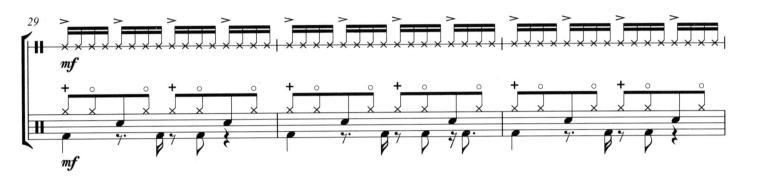

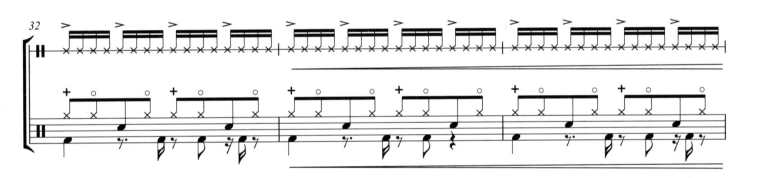

Tamb. down,
take stick

Bell of cymbal

HH

You may photocopy this page to avoid a page turn.

7evens

Pete Riley

Remember to look at the Performance Notes on pages 5-6

Swiss Swagger

Troy Miller

Remember to look at the Performance Notes on pages 5-6

Super High Five

Mark Schulman

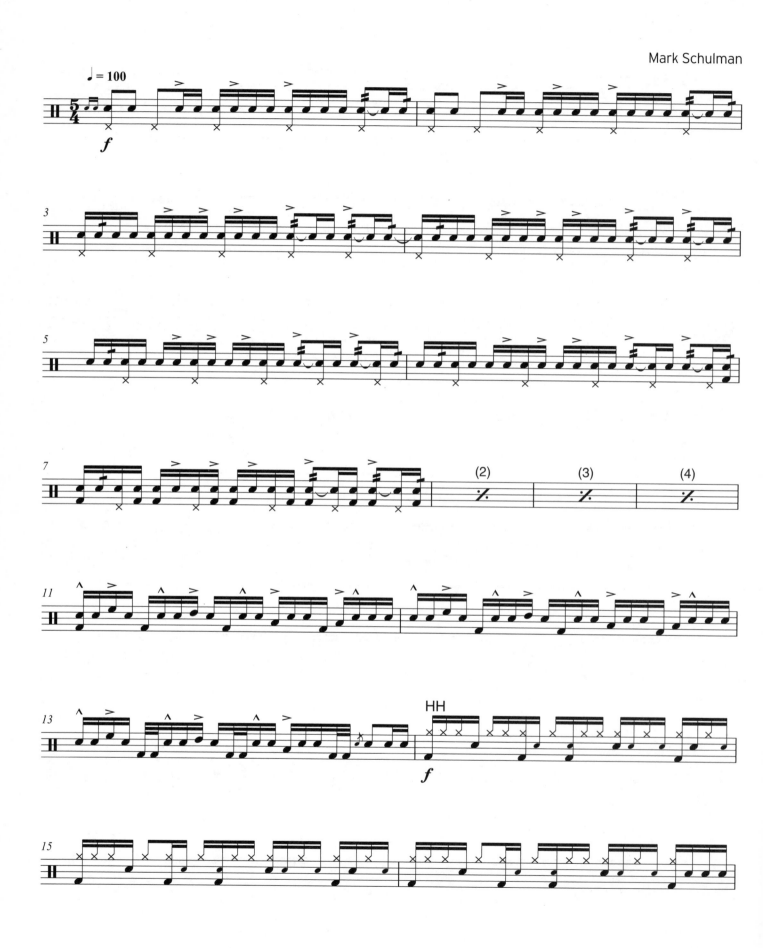

Remember to look at the Performance Notes on pages 5-6

* = Two Crash cymbals

You may photocopy this page to avoid a page turn.